## Publishing Credits

Dona Herweck Rice, *Editor-in-Chief*
Lee Aucoin, *Creative Director*
Kristy Stark, M.A.Ed., *Senior Editor*
Torrey Maloof, *Editor*
Kristine Magnien, M.S.Ed., *Associate Education Editor*
Neri Garcia, *Senior Designer*
Stephanie Reid, *Photo Researcher*
Rachelle Cracchiolo, M.S.Ed., *Publisher*

## Image Credits

p20: iStockphoto; all other images Shutterstock.

## Teacher Created Materials

5301 Oceanus Drive
Huntington Beach, CA 92649-1030
http://www.tcmpub.com
**ISBN 978-1-4333-4773-3**
© 2013 Teacher Created Materials, Inc.

# Table of Contents

D1455841

# Dear Family,

Welcome to third grade, a year that is full of fun! Students at this age usually enjoy school, having mastered most of the routines and having acquired many of the basic skills. Your child will explore reading longer books this year. Your child might need to prepare book reports. And get ready to practice those multiplication tables! You will probably find yourself helping with school projects for science and social studies, too.

If your third grader hasn't changed schools, he or she should have some close friends by now. That always makes school more fun. If your child is new to the school, making friends will be important. After-school time gets busier, but your child is also ready to assume more responsibility for his or her after-school activities. Fortunately, most third graders love school—and still love their teacher. You can help solidify that relationship by staying involved, too.

We know you are a busy parent, perhaps with other children and a job outside the home. This parent guide is organized to give you ideas that you can adapt to make the day smoother and to integrate learning into your routines.

## One last thought...

Your child may seem old enough to be very independent. But he or she still needs adults—parents, grandparents, or caretakers—who are working together to ensure that grade three is a year of learning and fun!

# A Good
## Start at Home

Your third grader's teacher will expect students to take responsibility for remembering homework, returning forms, and reminding parents to look over these items. Third graders will be expected to manage their materials efficiently.

*Try these ideas* to help your child be organized and responsible.

### In- and Out-Boxes

Have a place for everything. Create simple in- and out-boxes where homework, field trip, and permission slip papers that need immediate parent attention can be placed.

## Schedule It

Take time to set up a schedule together. Post the schedule for your child and caregivers to check.

## Time It

Your child can tell time by now, but you can still use a timer so that you don't have to be the timekeeper.

## Don't Delay

Encourage your child to take care of tasks promptly.

SCHEDULE

| 4:00 | Snack |
| 4:30 | Piano practice |
| 5:00 | Set the table, feed the dog |
| 5:30 | Dinner |
| 6:30 | Homework and reading time |
| 7:15 | Free time (after homework) |
| 7:45 | Get ready for bed |

## One last thought...

There will certainly be times when you can't maintain the nightly schedule. However, your child will thrive on whatever routine is possible to maintain.

# Homework
## Central

Your third grader may be expected to complete 30 minutes of homework each night. Forming good work habits should be a priority at this age.

• • • • • • • • • • • • • • • • • • • • • • • • • • • • • • • • • • •

*These tips will help* lay a foundation of a goo work ethic for your third grader.

### Nightly Homework

Make homework a nightly priority. Everyone in the family can work quie or read around the kitchen table dur homework time.

## Be Prepared

Your third grader will be learning many new concepts this year, such as multiplication facts. Make or buy flash cards and practice them each night for a few minutes.

## Good Guidance

Your child will sometimes need help with homework. Be the guide on the side and give help as needed.

## Role Model

Model good work habits. Catch up on your own work while your child does his or her homework.

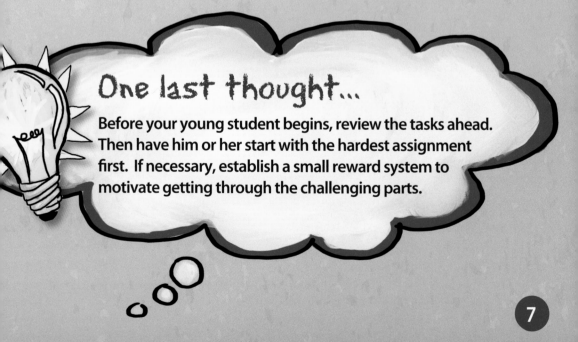

## One last thought...

Before your young student begins, review the tasks ahead. Then have him or her start with the hardest assignment first. If necessary, establish a small reward system to motivate getting through the challenging parts.

# Talk
## It Up!

Your child may need some time after school to decompress—it's hard to talk on demand. However, third graders still like talking about school and friends, even if it takes them a while to get started.

. . . . . . . . . . . . . . . . . . . . . . . . . . . . .

## *The following ideas can help* keep the conversations going.

### Conversation Starters

- What was one interesting thing you learned today?

- Who helped you at school today?

- Who is your favorite adult at school besides your teacher? The librarian? The principal?

### Humorous Happenings

Start the conversation during dinner preparations by talking about some funny things that happened during your day. Your humorous stories can serve as a conversational bridge during dinner.

What surprised you most about your day?

# One last thought...

Encourage your child to write down funny things you see. It gives you something to talk about at dinner! And don't worry if English isn't your first language. This is just about having fun with words!

# Sleep
## Smarter

Third graders need lots of sleep. Routine is the key word when it comes to establishing healthy sleep patterns. Take some time to think about the patterns that are in place. A new school year is a great time to improve them.

**The chart below shows how much sleep children need**

| Age | Sleep Needed |
|---|---|
| 1–3 years | 12–14 hours |
| 3–5 years | 11–13 hours |
| 5–12 years | 10–11 hours |

*These tips will help* your third grader get enough sleep.

### Keep Cool
Make sure your child's bedroom is cool, dark, and quiet.

### Exercise During the Day
Playing for at least three hours before bed helps your child get ready for sleep. These three hours can be spread out throughout the day!

### Keep the Routine
Have your child do the same relaxing things before bed each night, like taking a warm shower or reading. Your child's body will know it's time to get ready to sleep.

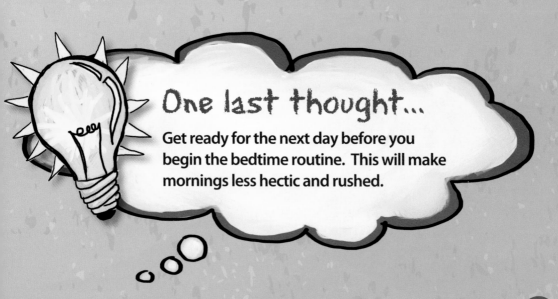

## One last thought...
Get ready for the next day before you begin the bedtime routine. This will make mornings less hectic and rushed.

# Top 10

## Things Your Third Grader
### Needs to Know

1. **Word identification strategies** when reading new words (e.g., root words, chunks, prefixes, suffixes)

2. **Ways language is used in writing** (e.g., similes, metaphors, personification, imagery)

3. **Research skills** such as using encyclopedias, nonfiction books, and the Internet for a research project

4. **Multiplication and division** within 100

5. **Fractions**

6. Area and perimeter of **one-dimensional shapes**

7. The **water cycle**

8. **Earth** is one of several planets that orbit the sun and that the moon orbits Earth

9. **Ideas about the government,** civic life, and politics

10. **Selective societies** in Africa, the Americas, Asia, and Europe

# Word
## Play

By now, your child is probably quite good at telling a joke. Puns, knock-knock jokes, or anything with a punch line are all fair game. Play with language whenever you can!

• • • • • • • • • • • • • • • • • • • • • • • • • • • • • • • •

*These word games will help* your third grader build his or her understanding of word meanings.

### Tongue Twisters

Tongue twisters occur when a beginning consonant or vowel in neighboring words is repeated within a phrase or sentence. For example, _now_ or _never_, _Peter Piper picked peppers_.

### Palindrome

A palindrome is a word or phrase that is read the same forward and backward. For example, *mom, kayak,* and *radar.*

kayak

## Pig Latin

With pig latin, the initial consonant sound of each word is moved to the end and *–ay* is added after it. However, when the words begin with a vowel, the initial sound isn't moved and *–ay* is added at the end. For example, the sentence *pig latin is fun* would be *ig-pay atin-lay is-ay un-fay*.

## Spoonerism

Spoonerisms occur when sounds are switched in a triangle of words with a humorous effect. For example, *butterfly—flutterby; go and take a shower—go and shake a tower*; and *save the whales—wave the sails*.

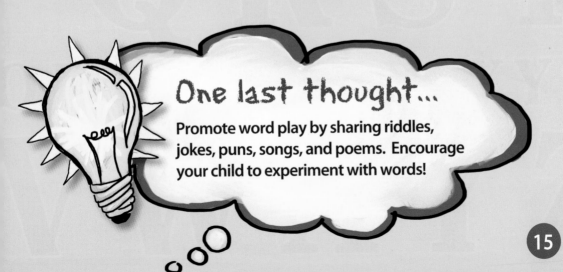

# One last thought...

Promote word play by sharing riddles, jokes, puns, songs, and poems. Encourage your child to experiment with words!

# Reading
## Rules!

Your third grader will be expected to make a huge leap in his or her fluency and understanding. At this stage, he or she should be able to read a variety books, including historical fiction, legends, fables, myths, and biographies.

*Use the following guidelines* to help improve your third grader's reading skills.

### Shared Reading

Set a reading time for the entire family. Take turns reading aloud or silently, or catching up on magazines.

## ...ook of the Month

...eate a family award for the best book of the month. Take turns ...ading an assortment of books and vote on which ones have the ...st writing or illustrations.

## ...omics

...ncourage your child to read the comics from the newspaper or ...ck up a comic book. Share the best cartoons with the ...mily. Discuss what makes them funny.

## ...agazines

...ubscribe to a magazine that expands your ...ild's interests, such as *National Geographic ...ids* or *Zoobooks*.

## ...ook Project

...ave your child create a project that represents ...recently read book: a map, drawings of costumes, ...poster, a postcard, stage setting, or illustrations.

## One last thought...

**Read aloud every day, even if it is just for ten minutes at the end of the day. This will help your child improve his or her reading skills.**

# What to Read?

Your third grader should be reading fewer picture books and filling the shelves with chapter books. Involve your child in assessing and organizing his or her book collection.

. . . . . . . . . . . . . . . . . . . . . . . . . . . .

**Here are some great reads for your third grader.**

- *Beezus and Ramona* by Beverly Cleary

- *Charlotte's Web* by E. B. White

- *Super Fudge* by Judy Blume

- *Captain Underpants* by Dav Pilkey

- *Cowgirl Kate and Cocoa* by Erica Silverman

- *A Bat is Born* by Randall Jarrell

- *Knoxville, Tennessee* by Nikki Giovanni

- *Weather* by Eve Merriam

- *Eating While Reading* by Gary Soto

Here are some ideas for how to find books.

- Library book sales

- Garage sales

- Sales at bookstores

- Swap books with neighbors

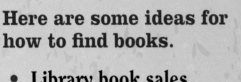

## One last thought...

Organize a book swap and consider trading in picture books for chapter books with friends and family.

# Spelling
## Strategies

Third graders are expected to write with accuracy. Teaching them a variety of strategies to help them correctly spell words by themselves is essential at this age.

## You can learn together
### and have fun with these ideas!

### Patterns

There are common spelling patterns. If your child knows how to spell one word, he or she can spell other words that follow the same pattern.

## Spelling Endings

There are a few spelling rules that will help. Keep these useful rules handy.

Does the word end in a silent *e*? Drop the *e* before adding *ing* or *y*.

**like** ⟶ **liking**    **nose** ⟶ **nosy**

Is the word one syllable, ending in one consonant? Double the consonant and add the ending.

**bed** ⟶ **bedding**    **hop** ⟶ **hopped**

Is the word one syllable, ending in two consonants? Or does it have two vowels in a row? Just add the ending.

**jump** ⟶ **jumping**    **peel** ⟶ **peeled**

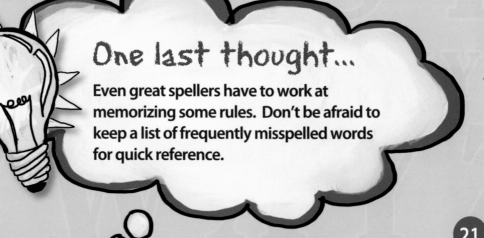

## One last thought...

Even great spellers have to work at memorizing some rules. Don't be afraid to keep a list of frequently misspelled words for quick reference.

# Common
## Prefixes and Suffixes

Here are some common prefixes and suffixes your child should know. Try putting these on flash cards to help your child memorize them!

| Prefix | Meaning | Examples |
| --- | --- | --- |
| mis- | wrongly | mistake, misbehave, misunderstand |
| un- | not | unhappy, unwanted, untie |
| pro- | favor, forward | proceed, progress, project |
| re- | again, back | redo, reuse, rewrite |
| pre- | before | preschool, prehistoric, preheat |

| Suffix | Meaning | Examples |
| --- | --- | --- |
| -ed | past tense | wanted, played, jumped |
| -er | more | bigger, smaller, taller |
| -est | most | biggest, smallest, tallest |
| -ing | present tense | playing, throwing, crying |
| -ly | like | friendly, quickly, sadly |
| -y | being or having | rainy, funny, bumpy |
| -less | without | thoughtless, careless, fearless |
| -ful | full of | careful, hopeful, joyful |

# Math
## at Home

Multiplication plays a big role in third grade, setting the stag for learning division. Your chil will also be doing more with fractions and geometry. Your home is a natural environmen for helping your child practice these concepts.

*Here are a few ideas* for using math in the kitchen.

### How Many?
Have your child figure out how many boxes of cake mix it will take to make cupcakes if there are 24 people coming to a party.

### Measure It
Involve your child in cooking the family dinner. You can have your child help you by measuring the ingredients. This is a great way to teach about liquid and dry measures.

### Double It
Have your child help you plan a big dinner. He or she can help by doubling the recipe.

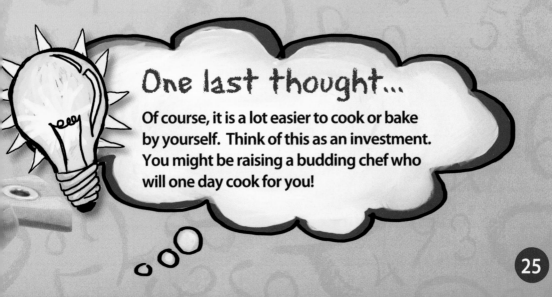

## One last thought...
Of course, it is a lot easier to cook or bake by yourself. Think of this as an investment. You might be raising a budding chef who will one day cook for you!

# Math Rules!

Third grade is the time to get the rules of math firmly in place. Your child will be working on solving addition, subtraction, multiplication, and division problems with a deeper understanding of how everything relates.

## These ideas may help when math homework time comes.

### Be Strategic

To solve a word problem, read it aloud two or three times. Is it still too hard? Substitute big numbers with smaller numbers or draw a picture.

### Use Tools

Math is more than rote memorization. Use these tools to help understand the problem at hand: counting blocks or toothpicks to show groups of tens, a ruler, coins, etc.

### Follow These Steps:

1. Study the examples.

2. Work or explain the examples.

3. Work the problems (encourage legible numbers).

4. Check the work.

## One last thought...

Processes change, so offer the way you learned as a child as one way of several. Then ask your child to explain how he or she has been taught. Through the explanation, your child will gain a better understanding of both techniques.

# Multiplication
## and Division Facts

Mastering multiplication and division is a part of third grade math.  Help your child conquer this feat by practicing his or her math facts every day!  T putting multiplication facts on flash cards to help memorize them.

|    | 0 | 1 | 2 | 3 | 4 |
|----|---|---|---|---|---|
| 0  | 0 | 0 | 0 | 0 | 0 |
| 1  | 0 | 1 | 2 | 3 | 4 |
| 2  | 0 | 2 | 4 | 6 | 8 |
| 3  | 0 | 3 | 6 | 9 | 12 |
| 4  | 0 | 4 | 8 | 12 | 16 |
| 5  | 0 | 5 | 10 | 15 | 20 |
| 6  | 0 | 6 | 12 | 18 | 24 |
| 7  | 0 | 7 | 14 | 21 | 28 |
| 8  | 0 | 8 | 16 | 24 | 32 |
| 9  | 0 | 9 | 18 | 27 | 36 |
| 10 | 0 | 10 | 20 | 30 | 40 |

| 5 | 6 | 7 | 8 | 9 | 10 |
|---|---|---|---|---|---|
| 0 | 0 | 0 | 0 | 0 | 0 |
| 5 | 6 | 7 | 8 | 9 | 10 |
| 10 | 12 | 14 | 16 | 18 | 20 |
| 15 | 18 | 21 | 24 | 27 | 30 |
| 20 | 24 | 28 | 32 | 36 | 40 |
| 25 | 30 | 35 | 40 | 45 | 50 |
| 30 | 36 | 42 | 48 | 54 | 60 |
| 35 | 42 | 49 | 56 | 63 | 70 |
| 40 | 48 | 56 | 64 | 72 | 80 |
| 45 | 54 | 63 | 72 | 81 | 90 |
| 50 | 60 | 70 | 80 | 90 | 100 |

# Science
## Fun!

Third graders will be exploring more about Earth and the life-forms that inhabit it. They will also learn about the water cycle. That is what third grad is all about—understanding how things react, combine, reform, and change

*These activities will help* your child to explore and think more critically.

### Animal Habitats

Have your third grader build a habitat. Fill an aquarium with one inch of mud. Collect pond water and let it sit in direct sunlight for a few days. Next, slowly add the pond water to the aquarium through a strainer. Once the aquarium is set up, ad tadpoles or other insects.

## Kitchen Science

Learn about density by layering liquids. Slowly pour vegetable oil, water mixed with food coloring, and rubbing alcohol into a clear container. Watch the denser liquids sink!

## Investigate

If a plant dies, try to figure out the cause. Not enough water? Too much water? Encourage your child to think like an investigator.

## Water Cycle

Fill a clear cup with water. Place plastic wrap on top of the cup and seal with a rubber band. Place in the sun and watch precipitation form.

## One last thought...

Your third grader probably still likes to make messes—even in the dirt! There is a lot of learning going on, so just enjoy the mess. And then help your inventor do the clean up!

# Exploring
## Social Studies

Third graders are learning about our country and early explorers.
Help your child discover more about the world around him or her,
especially beyond the home.

*Use the following activities* to engage
your child in ideas about civic life, politics, and
the government.

### Newspaper
The daily newspaper is the perfect ongoing history lesson.

- Use the ads to discuss the impact
  of seasonal trends and sales on
  the economy.

- Read the sections about local
  citizens, this day in history, and
  community announcements.

- Read the editorial cartoons or
  follow local politics.

## Family History

By this year, your budding historian may be expected to contribute to a whole-class project by cooking or creating art. This is a good time to connect your child with your family's traditions including foods, clothing, and holidays.

## Good Citizens

Take a walk through your courthouse or city hall and discuss how your local government works—its laws and the roles of citizens.

## One last thought...

This is the perfect year to explore your family's history. Consider having your third grader interview a grandparent or great-grandparent to experience some oral history.

# *Balancing*
## School and Beyond

Your third grader may be ready for more organized group activities after school or on the weekends. Alternatively, he or she may need time to decompress after a busy day.

. . . . . . . . . . . . . . . . . . . . . . . . . . . . . . . . . . . . . . .

*Here are some ideas* to help your child balance school and beyond.

### Community Center
Check out your local community center for a variety of classes designed for kids. Oftentimes they are offered at discounted prices!

### Art Fair
Check your city's programs to see if any art fairs or events are scheduled. This would be a great time to expose your child to different kinds of art!

### Library Program
Many libraries have programs especially for kids. Look into getting a library card for your child and have him or her get involved at your local library.

### School Clubs
Your student's school may offer after-school clubs, such as the chess club, Spanish club, or cooking club.

## One last thought...

Your child may be enthusiastic about all kinds of programs, only to declare he or she is ready to quit after a few classes or practices. Ease into long-term commitments so that the risk of frustration, disappointment, or wasted fees is minimized.

# Learning
## on the Go

Whether you are taking a short or long trip, take advantage of this time by linking your trips to the community and its history.

• • • • • • • • • • • • • • • • • • • • • • • • • • • •

*Use these recommendations* to take advantage of learning on the go.

### Be Prepared

Seek information about a city from the local chamber of commerce. Explore things to see and the history of the area. If you aren't going on a trip, pretend to be a first-time visitor in your own community.

### Photographer

Invest in a digital camera to record the trip.

### Fortunately-Unfortunately

This is a fun storytelling game. Each person makes up a sentence in the story, alternating between fortunate and unfortunate events.

### Read Aloud

Have one person (who is not subject to carsickness) read aloud from a chapter book, a travel guide, or a magazine. Audio books are great for car travel, too.

# One last thought...

Put together a travel bag or backpack that holds a variety of materials such as markers, crayons, paper on a clipboard, and word puzzles.

# Staying
## Playful

You may feel like these years are all about studying and mastering skills. Research tells us, however, that play is always important. Through group games, we learn to think strategically, solve problems, and even get some exercise.

# *Try some* of these fun games.

### Rainy Day Games
Play old classics such as Musical Chairs, Hot Potato, Guess that Drawing, or Charades.

### Outdoor Games
Have your child join the neighborhood children with adult supervision and play some outdoor games such as kickball or Capture the Flag.

### Yard Game
Scatter several plastic hoops around the yard. Assign taggers to freeze the other players. Children inside a plastic hoop cannot get frozen, but can only stay long enough to count to 10. Only one child per plastic hoop is allowed.

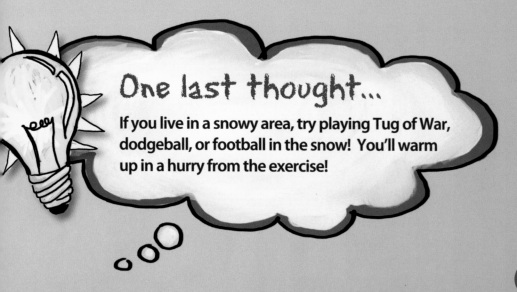

## One last thought...
If you live in a snowy area, try playing Tug of War, dodgeball, or football in the snow! You'll warm up in a hurry from the exercise!

Your third grader is becoming more independent in so many ways. Third graders are more confident and curious about everything. It's an exciting stage, and you have so much to explore with your child! We hope this collection of ideas will make the year even better. Than you for taking the time to browse through them.

Remember, you don't have to be a "super" parent (or grandparent every minute of the day. Be ready to learn some new things with you child and take time to have fun, too!

*Thank you!*